1 & 2
Thessalonians

GARY R. SMALL

1 & 2 THESSALONIANS
Copyright © 2023 by Gary R. Small

Print ISBN: 978-1-4866-2396-9
eBook ISBN: 978-1-4866-2397-6

Word Alive Press
119 De Baets Street, Winnipeg, MB R2J 3R9
www.wordalivepress.ca

WORD ALIVE
—P R E S S—

Cataloguing in Publication may be obtained through Library and Archives Canada

Contents

Series Introduction

Keep this Book of the Law always on your lips; meditate on it day and night, so that you may be careful to do everything written in it. Then you will be prosperous and successful.
—Joshua 1:8

The word meditate and its derivatives occur eighteen times in the Bible. Of these, eight pertain to meditating on the Scriptures. Through these verses, we are encouraged to hold God's word in our hearts so that we might profit from His wisdom and be blessed by a closer relationship with Him (Psalm 119:1–3).

The secular world has also proposed the concept of taking a thoughtful approach to life and uses the word mindfulness to describe a thoughtful, meditative approach to life.

Mindfulness has been defined as "the awareness that arises through paying attention in the present moment, on purpose, non-judgmentally."[1] Other terms have been applied to this intentional

---

1 Judson Brewer, *Unwinding Anxiety* (New York, NY: Avery, 2021), 71. Quoting Jon Kabat-Zinn.

approach, such as *to internalize, to meditate on,* or *to process.* It is what we as Christians do when we carefully consider the Bible.

The trouble is that we often don't have time to study in this manner. Instead we find ourselves snatching moments in our busy lives to read, internalize, and digest passages from our daily reading of the Bible. By squeezing these most important moments of the day into the least number of minutes, we don't make time for the mindfulness required to truly digest God's word.

Another mistake we often fall into is having too high expectations of ourselves. We lean into weighty commentaries or topical novels on life-changing subjects and once again find that we don't have the sufficient time or headspace to do justice to the meaty subjects therein.

We previously referred to this problem as having too much pace and not sufficient peace to make sense of God's word. It is the challenge that led to the production of this series of books, which are designed to help lift a word from His word and make it poignant.

How we choose to use the selected word for each chapter will be different for each reader. Each chapter is designed to provoke mindful thought on a biblical passage. We have also provided three applications at the end of each chapter to stimulate further reflection.

It is hoped that the chosen word from each passage will be recalled throughout the day when we find moments of stillness or thought, so we can pay attention, on purpose, nonjudgmentally.

These books can be used by individuals. They may also find use in group settings to provoke further discussion on a sermon series or in small group Bible study.

It is hoped that the books will be used as a spiritual tool to reinvigorate your Bible reading and provide the impetus to make a life change as a Christian.

The concept is simple, one which by no means seeks to detract from the value of in-depth Bible study. There is still a place for this when time allows and further reading references are provided. We have taken care to tread a middle road theologically and avoid weighty arguments on some finer points of hermeneutics, although some of these can be found within the referenced material.

We sincerely hope that *A Word from His Word* will not only lift selected words from the pages of Scripture but also provide a lift to your Bible reading and spiritual life.

Much has been made by the secular world of the benefits of mindfulness. I suspect this discipline is not new, although it has perhaps been lost in our striving for scientific purpose. Yet there is, in this series, an opportunity to rediscover the usefulness of intentional meditation on God's word (Psalm 1:1–2).

Foreword

It is a great privilege to be asked to write a foreword for *A Word from His word: Thessalonians*. I met Gary ten years ago through a church house group that he shepherded and I hosted. It was an active group full of friends and neighbours from our church.

Gary's great love for the word is inspirational. His material was always well-researched and supported by his enthusiasm for God's word. It was easy to be affected by his enthusiasm. Over a period of four years, we studied many topical studies and worked our way through several books of the Bible.

I appreciated reading this edition from the series. It reminded me of our Bible studies with Gary. I found myself thinking of his enthusiasm and illustrations from our sessions. His writing style has glimpses of this energy and positive optimism for the promises of God's word. This led me back to consider the text and ponder on the words which seemed richer for having been dwelt on.

I sincerely believe you will also appreciate this short devotional. You will no doubt reflect on the words and find yourself considering some of the applications and illustrations. I hope that it will help to bring the Thessalonian church back to life and that the Holy Spirit will help you experience the truth of His word for you personally today.

May you be blessed by reading this thoughtful book.

—Bob Auld
Lay Leader, Spiritual Formation Ministry
Thunder Bay, Ontario

Introduction

1 THESSALONIANS

Acts 16–17:10 shares the historical account of how Paul, Silas, and Timothy came to arrive in Thessalonica (modern-day Thessaloniki) and how they came to leave.

During Paul's second missionary journey (AD 49–50), he travelled to Macedonia and established churches in major cities. Thessalonica was a large port city in Macedonia and provided the Roman Empire with access to the east. Being a port, it was influenced by many different cultures and is thought to have accommodated believers of Egyptian, Greek, and Roman gods as well as a synagogue for the Jews.

Paul is believed to have written his first letter to the Thessalonians not long after his departure, around AD 52. It is thought to have been written from a position of relative comfort for Paul during his stay in Corinth. His early correspondence was perhaps a reflection of the short time he spent there and his concern that the new converts to Christianity not feel abandoned.

Contrary to Paul's concerns, however, he had received reports from Timothy that the church in Thessalonica was surviving despite persecution and some challenging issues.

It is interesting to note that although Thessalonica was only ninety miles away from Philippi, the controversies that had arisen in the congregation were quite different from those of the Philippians. The unique challenges likely reflected the eclectic mix of believers in Thessalonica. The multiplicity of faith backgrounds, for example, had created the unusual circumstances wherein Paul found himself having to remind the church to take care of their physical needs and not become so preoccupied with the return of Christ.

In modern times, the pendulum has possibly swung too far on this point: we are too occupied with physical needs that we have no time to address our spiritual ones. Arguably, this is why this book is relevant. 1 Thessalonians calls us to recentre our faith, to recall our initial conversion and our pastoring by those who ministered to us. As we are recalled back to that original path, we will find harmony in our daily physical duties and our spiritual disciplines. At least, this is what we hope will happen as you read this edition of A Word from His Word.

Imitators

1 THESSALONIANS 1:1–10

Paul, Silas and Timothy,

To the church of the Thessalonians in God the Father and the Lord Jesus Christ: Grace and peace to you.

[2] We always thank God for all of you and continually mention you in our prayers. [3] We remember before our God and Father your work produced by faith, your labor prompted by love, and your endurance inspired by hope in our Lord Jesus Christ.

[4] For we know, brothers and sisters loved by God, that he has chosen you, [5] because our gospel came to you not simply with words but also with power, with the Holy Spirit and deep conviction. You know how we lived among you for your sake. [6] You became imitators of us and of the Lord, for you welcomed the message in the midst of severe suffering with the joy given by the Holy Spirit. [7] And so you became a model to all the believers in Macedonia and Achaia. [8] The Lord's message rang out from you not only in Macedonia and Achaia—your faith in God has become known everywhere. Therefore we do not need to say anything about it, [9] for they themselves report what kind of reception

you gave us. They tell how you turned to God from idols to serve the living and true God, [10] and to wait for his Son from heaven, whom he raised from the dead—Jesus, who rescues us from the coming wrath.

In these introductory verses, Paul is effusive in his praise and encouragement toward the church in Thessalonica. One of the attributes about them he affirms is their imitation of Paul, Silas, and Timothy (1 Thessalonians 1:6). The word imitators is translated from the Greek *mimetes*, which means "to follow or copy the behaviour of another." This is the root of such words as mime or pantomime. We might picture a mime artist copying or performing choreographed moves to demonstrate emotion or an activity.

What impressed Paul and his co-authors was the manner in which the Thessalonian believers mirrored the behaviours witnessed to them. In particular, they were pleased to hear that the Thessalonians had adopted God-centred (1 Thessalonians 1:9), joyous (1 Thessalonians 1:6), and evangelical (1 Thessalonians 1:8) lives.

Paul is mindful to acknowledge that it is a huge step to become theocentric and believe in God. The cosmopolitan Thessalonians were surrounded by multiple gods from multiple ancient cultures, and as such many had a new age approach to religion, selecting different aspects of different faiths to suit their own needs. Paul congratulates them on being open to receiving the news of God the Father and turning from idols to serve Him (1 Thessalonians 1:9).

The Thessalonians had reflected what they'd observed in Paul and his colleagues to make God a centrepiece of their faith and draw on His resources rather than rely on their own in their everyday lives (1 Thessalonians 1:8).

We should pause to consider whether we, in modern society, tend to see life through the lens of technology and man-created solutions without a reliance or reference to God. Our challenge as Christians in the twenty-first century is to continue to imitate the attitudes of the apostles and use God as a foundation to demonstrate our faith.

APPLICATION: IMITATORS

- Pray that your lifestyle will resonate with the gospel, imitating its message so that others can be encouraged.
- Do you leave room for God to help in your making decisions? Reaffirm your reliance on Him.
- Thank God for inspiring individuals you can imitate from Scripture or from real life.

Witness

You know, brothers and sisters, that our visit to you was not without results. ² We had previously suffered and been treated outrageously in Philippi, as you know, but with the help of our God we dared to tell you his gospel in the face of strong opposition. ³ For the appeal we make does not spring from error or impure motives, nor are we trying to trick you. ⁴ On the contrary, we speak as those approved by God to be entrusted with the gospel. We are not trying to please people but God, who tests our hearts. ⁵ You know we never used flattery, nor did we put on a mask to cover up greed—God is our witness. ⁶ We were not looking for praise from people, not from you or anyone else, even though as apostles of Christ we could have asserted our authority. ⁷ Instead, we were like young children among you.

Just as a nursing mother cares for her children, ⁸ so we cared for you. Because we loved you so much, we were delighted to share with you not only the gospel of God but our lives as well. ⁹ Surely you remember, brothers and sisters, our toil and hardship; we worked night and day in order not to be a burden to anyone while we preached the gospel of God to you. [10] You are witnesses, and so is God, of how holy, righteous and blameless we were among you who believed. [11] For you know that we dealt with each of you as a father deals with his own children, [12] encouraging, comforting and urging you to live lives worthy of God, who calls you into his kingdom and glory.

In these verses, Paul continues to acknowledge the remarkable progress the Thessalonians had made. He highlights how the message the Thessalonians heard was witnessed by God (1 Thessalonians 2:5 and 10).

The significance of having a witness may be lost in the twenty-first century. In our modern world of close-circuit television, social media, and twenty-four-hour news coverage, it's easy to forget that there was a time when the only witnesses were those who saw events in person. Now, even in the absence of direct witnesses, someone is always watching through a live stream or recording.

Paul ministered at a time before such technologies existed and he takes time to remind the Thessalonians that someone was watching his teaching amongst them. God Himself was a witness to the gospel message brought by Timothy, Silas, and Paul (1 Thessalonians 2:5).

Paul again stresses the importance of having God as a witness in 1 Thessalonians 2:10, and witness will be our word to focus on from theses verses. Paul emphasized the concept of God as his witness since he wished to underline the authenticity of the apostles' message.

In a port city like Thessalonica, which was open to sea traffic from throughout the Mediterranean basin, the population was exposed to a number of charlatans and peddlers seeking their own fame and fortune. In contrast, Paul didn't preach his message for worldly gain; rather, he was tasked by God to call his hearers into His kingdom and glory (1 Thessalonians 2:12).

Paul highlights that the ministry team didn't work for their own sakes but rather to bring the good news of God's outreach to communities who had not seen or heard of Jesus. He sought to encourage the Thessalonians to continue to operate with God as their witness, especially in the realm of evangelism and outreach.

Being in God's presence, His spotlight, can be unnerving. Although once we remember that it is He who called us (1 Thessalonians 2:12) and reflect on the parental roles Paul describes, being in His presence seems less like being caught in the glare of a spotlight and more like sailing under the guiding light of a lighthouse.

Be mindful today that we practice our Christianity in the witness of God and let this thought motivate our own witness to be pure, like Paul's.

APPLICATION: WITNESS

- How does it feel to think of God as being a witness of our lives?
- Be encouraged to accept this with a positive analogy, like the example of a lighthouse at sea.
- Thank God that He wishes to walk with you as a witness, that you might live a life worthy of His calling.

Received and Accepted

1 THESSALONIANS 2:13-16

And we also thank God continually because, when you received the word of God, which you heard from us, you accepted it not as a human word, but as it actually is, the word of God, which is indeed at work in you who believe. [14] For you, brothers and sisters, became imitators of God's churches in Judea, which are in Christ Jesus: You suffered from your own people the same things those churches suffered from the Jews [15] who killed the Lord Jesus and the prophets and also drove us out. They displease God and are hostile to everyone [16] in their effort to keep us from speaking to the Gentiles so that they may be saved. In this way they always heap up their sins to the limit. The wrath of God has come upon them at last.

Paul continues to celebrate the amazing transformation that the Thessalonian Christians had undergone. From pagan beliefs or Hellenized Judaism, the new Christian community had come to accept Paul's teachings regarding Jesus. This miraculous transition had occurred following the briefest of missions.

Paul, Silas, and Timothy had spoken for three sabbaths in the synagogue, and perhaps a while longer in non-synagogue ministry, but their visit was cut short (Acts 17). As a testimony to the strength of their teaching, the consistency of their lifestyles, and the power of God's word, the lives of the Thessalonians had been radically altered.

We can be sure of their dramatic change in perspective from non-Christian to Christian given Paul's absolute delight and congratulations. Paul is especially delighted to note the consistency with which the Thessalonians were persisting in their new beliefs.

Paul writes that the Thessalonians received and accepted the Word of God (1 Thessalonians 2:13). In this verse, he communicates something of the weight with which God's word should be received.

We will consider the words receive and accept from this passage. *Paralambano* is the Greek word translated as received. It speaks to the taking of what is being given in a practical or physical sense. *Dechomai* was the Greek word translated as accepted and communicates the processing or comprehension of what was said. In English, we might use accepted for both the practical taking and the mental comprehension of a gift, and in the process we might miss something of Paul's subtext.

As Christians, we often receive God's word but fail to accept it with an appropriate response. This thought was partially the driver for the Word from His Word series, wherein we allow ourselves the opportunity to focus on His word. In doing so, I have hoped that His word will be received and accepted with more meaning, translating into His word having greater influence in people's lives.

It was a source of encouragement to Paul for the Thessalonians to have experienced genuine conversion after such a short mission. This was also evidence that God's word had not only been taken in but been taken on, as something divine should be.

Paul contrasts the Thessalonian response to that of the Jews. Sadly, the Jews had failed to receive God's word of the gospel as a divine message.

Paul had some harsh words to say in 1 Thessalonians 2:15–16 regarding non-Christian Jews. In these verses, we must not lose sight of the fact that ultimately everyone is judged by God. As a Christian, only through appropriately receiving God's son are we saved from His wrath at judgment.

How comfortable are we about how appropriately we receive God's word? Is it given the weight of influence or time that is due, or are we guilty of paying it lip service? If God's word is to have the same influence on us as it had on the Thessalonians, we will have to consider our *paralambano* and *dechomai* responses, so that we will be both more attentive and receptive of His teachings.

APPLICATION:
RECEIVED AND ACCEPTED

- Reflect on a piece of advice that had an impact on your life. What was it about the advice that made you receive and accept it?

- Do you consider God's word to be spoken with divine authority? Consider your response to His word in light of the Thessalonian example.
- Take time to thank God for His word and pray that it may affect you anew.

Strengthen and Encourage

But, brothers and sisters, when we were orphaned by being separated from you for a short time (in person, not in thought), out of our intense longing we made every effort to see you. [18] For we wanted to come to you—certainly I, Paul, did, again and again—but Satan blocked our way. [19] For what is our hope, our joy, or the crown in which we will glory in the presence of our Lord Jesus when he comes? Is it not you? [20] Indeed, you are our glory and joy.

[1] So when we could stand it no longer, we thought it best to be left by ourselves in Athens. [2] We sent Timothy, who is our brother and co-worker in God's service in spreading the gospel of Christ, to strengthen and encourage you in your faith, [3] so that no one would be unsettled by these trials. For you know quite well that we are destined for them. [4] In fact, when we were with you, we kept telling you that we would be persecuted. And it turned out that way, as you well know. [5] For this reason, when I could stand it no longer, I sent to find out about your faith. I was afraid that in some way the

tempter had tempted you and that our labors might have been in vain.

⁶ But Timothy has just now come to us from you and has brought good news about your faith and love. He has told us that you always have pleasant memories of us and that you long to see us, just as we also long to see you. ⁷ Therefore, brothers and sisters, in all our distress and persecution we were encouraged about you because of your faith. ⁸ For now we really live, since you are standing firm in the Lord.

Do you often stop to consider what is your purpose in relation to other Christians? In today's reading, Paul gives some food for thought in this regard.

Concerned that the Thessalonian church may have wilted under the cultural and social pressures that besieged them, Paul and Silas sent Timothy back to learn the state of affairs. Specifically, Timothy returned to strengthen and encourage the early Christians so they would persevere and endure in their new faith (1 Thessalonians 3:2).

The Greek word for strengthen, *sterizo*, was commonly used to indicate supporting or stabilizing a structure. It could be applied in construction to refer to buttresses or supports that stabilized a wall.

Timothy was sent back to offer support to Thessalonians to help prevent the church from collapsing. The ministry team had a genuine concern that the church might crumble as it was pulled apart by persecution and social isolation.

The Greek word for encourage here is *parakaleo*. It is a construct of two words—*para*, which means "alongside," and *kaleo*, which translates as "to invite or call." To encourage was then to call someone alongside, as a cyclist might do to a teammate or a social runner during a jog. The presence of another person in close proximity can be motivating in those circumstances.

For Paul, having Timothy visit the Thessalonians and experience their lives was intended to encourage them through his support. When we encourage others, we are investing ourselves in their lives.

Encouragement involves giving time, thought, and perhaps personal discomfort in order to come alongside a person in a personal way. It speaks volumes of Timothy's character that he was selected for this role. Giving of oneself in this manner speaks to the heart of Christianity and the commandments highlighted by Jesus in Matthew 22:36–40.

Timothy went back to Thessalonica to call the early Christians to walk with him for a while in their new faith. As he did so, he sought to support them and stabilize the congregation.

Timothy was able to report to Paul that the Thessalonians were in fact thriving as a church. Their faith and persistence with the teachings of Paul, Timothy, and Silas underlined the genuine nature of their conversion and confirmed that they had truly received the Holy Spirit. This clearly made Timothy's job of support and encouragement easier, but his presence was still important.

In our twenty-first-century lives, we tend to have a performance-related mindset. We become accustomed through our schooling and sports that our value is intimately related to whether we achieve certain benchmarks. Such an approach has its merits as it can provide objective measures of progress when it comes to teaching or coaching points. In Paul's mind, the Thessalonians were achieving and practicing many of the disciplines he expected of young Christians.

A potential downside to focussing on performance is that it can create a critical atmosphere. As coaches, educators, or even pastoral leaders, we can place too much emphasis on critical appraisal. Rather than support and encourage our charges, such an emphasis can destabilize and discourage them. Critical appraisal that leads to destabilization and discouragement can have disastrous consequences for young and mature Christians.

In asking Timothy to return to Thessalonica to encourage and support, Paul employed a strategy that goes contrary to our modern techniques of performance evaluation. Paul stresses the importance of the personal invitation to come alongside others to encourage them. He writes that the purpose of Timothy's visit was to support, not destabilize—or worse, deconstruct—the early church.

Our challenge is to ensure that our interactions with fellow Christians are marked by support and encouragement. It is worthwhile to reflect on the opportunities we may have to be like Timothy to those who might benefit from our support and encouragement.

APPLICATION:
STRENGTHEN AND ENCOURAGE

- Thank God in prayer for those Christians who have provided you with support and encouragement.
- Consider those to whom you could offer support and encouragement. Pray for an opportunity to do so.
- Reflect on whether your attitudes and approach to other Christians seeks to support and encourage.

Enough

1 THESSALONIANS 3:9–13

How can we thank God enough for you in return for all the joy we have in the presence of our God because of you? [10] Night and day we pray most earnestly that we may see you again and supply what is lacking in your faith.

[11] Now may our God and Father himself and our Lord Jesus clear the way for us to come to you. [12] May the Lord make your love increase and overflow for each other and for everyone else, just as ours does for you. [13] May he strengthen your hearts so that you will be blameless and holy in the presence of our God and Father when our Lord Jesus comes with all his holy ones.

One of the challenges of the book of Thessalonians to Christians today is to promote more godly attitudes to our fellow Christians. As an example of this, in today's passage we will focus on the thought that Paul didn't feel that he could thank God enough for the Christians in Thessalonica.

Consider that Paul, perhaps one of the greatest theologians and evangelists, felt he was unable to find the words and emotions to express the enormity of his appreciation for the Thessalonian church!

The word translated as enough is *antapodidomi* and is a composite of *anti* and *apodidomi*. *Anti* means "in turn," and *apididomi* can be translated as "to return or give back." Paul is indicating that he was unable to sufficiently give thanks back to God for what He had done in the Thessalonian Christians.

Perhaps we might expect a lesser evangelist or missionary to feel such a debt to God, but in order to express this Paul indicates his humble acceptance that the work of God and the Holy Spirit must be respectfully honoured for any perceived successes of the Thessalonian church.

If this was Paul's attitude, should we not also feel a debt of gratitude to God for our fellow Christians? When was the last time we felt an inadequacy of resources to thank God for our brothers or sisters in Christ?

This is an arresting thought for Paul, Timothy, and Silas, as authors of this letter. It is also a challenge for us today: we should be more thankful to God for our fellow Christians. Paul encourages us to give thanks for both Christians we had the blessing to nurture, and for mature members of our church.

As a parent, this could be also be extended to expressing a debt of gratitude for the blessing of Christian children. Or as a child of Christians parents, you might be prompted to demonstrate your appreciation of them.

In addition to thanking God for the Thessalonians, Paul continues to pray for them. His prayer is a useful example of how we might express our thanks to God by continuing to pray for those Christians we know. Paul prays (1 Thessalonians 3:12–13) that their love for one another would continue to grow and asks that

17

they would be strengthened to be able walk in faith until such time as they stood before God.

Please take a moment to consider Paul, this great man of God, realizing that he was inadequate to thank God enough for the faith and persistence of the Thessalonians. Let these thoughts motivate your own thanks and prayers for the Christians you know, perhaps adapting Paul's own prayer to pray for them.

APPLICATION: ENOUGH

- Consider those who nurtured and discipled you as a Christian. Thank God for their grace and persistence.
- Thank God for those Christians you have been blessed to disciple and for those you currently pastor.
- Reflect with Paul on the debt of gratitude that is ours in the light of God's grace to maintain our brothers and sisters in Christ.

Sanctified

1 THESSALONIANS 4:1-8

As for other matters, brothers and sisters, we instructed you how to live in order to please God, as in fact you are living. Now we ask you and urge you in the Lord Jesus to do this more and more. [2] For you know what instructions we gave you by the authority of the Lord Jesus.

[3] It is God's will that you should be sanctified: that you should avoid sexual immorality; [4] that each of you should learn to control your own body in a way that is holy and honorable, [5] not in passionate lust like the pagans, who do not know God; [6] and that in this matter no one should wrong or take advantage of a brother or sister. The Lord will punish all those who commit such sins, as we told you and warned you before. [7] For God did not call us to be impure, but to live a holy life. [8] Therefore, anyone who rejects this instruction does not reject a human being but God, the very God who gives you his Holy Spirit.

Paul begins his discourse by using a particular type of rhetoric that seeks to affirm the behaviour of the Thessalonians and encourage them to pursue what they are already doing with greater vigour.

This is demonstrative rhetoric and should be contrasted against judicial rhetoric—judgmental commentary, or deliberate rhetoric, which relates to confrontational exhortation.

Paul's words in these verses are meant to gently encourage the Thessalonians to continue in their current vein to follow Christ and apply this in areas of their lives such as sexual practices.

Paul highlights the avoidance of sexual immorality, implying that failing to do so would undermine their sanctification. The word sanctification is translated here from the Greek *hagiasmos*, the stem of which is *hagios*, or holy. *Hagiasmos* speaks to an uncompleted process of purification or consecration. Sanctification is therefore a process, not a completed task. It is contrasted in 1 Thessalonians 4:7 with *akatharsia*, or impurity (1 Thessalonians 4:7), a more literal translation of which would be "without cleanliness."

Sexual behaviour is a sensitive topic. However, it was clearly important to Paul and had obviously been a concern to Timothy, who had returned to Paul with news of the Thessalonians. Precisely what aspects of sexual deviancy Timothy had particular concerns can only be guessed at. Paul stressed the importance of self-control, being honourable, and not being lustful. He also emphasized the impact of sexual immorality on others (1 Thessalonians 4:6). Paul was therefore keen for the Thessalonians to avoid personal and corporate consequences.

I suspect that sex was one of the "evil desires of youth" Timothy was exhorted to flee in 2 Timothy 2:22. It is probably true that whatever evil desires youth should flee from are also to be fled from by mature adults. Such evil desires do not become less evil as we age. Perhaps their allure lessens, but they are still to be avoided.

When it comes to sex, society has done an amazing job at clouding our impressions of what is holy and pure versus what is not. The indistinction between the two can make it easier to become embroiled in activities, relationships, and hobbies which might not be in our best interests as Christians.

It has been suggested by neuroscientist, psychiatrist, and writer Judson Brewer that a "bigger better offer" is required to usurp an addiction.[2] Such a prize encourages our reward-orientated minds to switch allegiance from a temporarily pleasing but long-term destructive behaviour to a habit with more edifying long-term results.

If Dr. Brewer is correct, the challenge for Christians is twofold. First, the prize of holiness may not seem like such a big reward. Second, the destructive nature of sexual impurity may not seem to be true.

To better explain the second of these comments let us contrast our perceptions of illicit drug use versus sexual impurity.

Public health messaging has been very clear concerning the destructive effect of illicit drugs. Pamphlets and public notices have shown harrowing images of emaciated youths, with arms littered with scars from needles and tract marks. There can be little doubt as to the destructive nature of this habit when we see thin

---

2 Judson Brewer Avery, *Unwinding Anxiety* (New York, NY: Penguin Random House, 2021), 164–165.

faces with hollowed-out eye sockets. In order for people to readily grasp the "bigger better offer" of pursing holiness, we might contrast such images with those of vibrant non-addicted youth.

Sexual impurity, however, is not viewed by our society as such an impropriety. Premarital sex, extramarital affairs, and other sexual practices are glamorized without reference to their destructive nature and the emotional scars they leave behind.

In order for sexual impurity to be viewed with the same horror as illicit drugs abuse, we must question both our own and our society's lackadaisical approach to sex. I'm not suggesting a radical shift to a monastic or convent lifestyle, but I would condone a more circumspect approach to what we accept as normal and reasonable behaviour.

God's standards in this area are high, and for meeting it He offers a "bigger better reward." It is my prayer that we would be willing to have our hearts and minds opened to the destructive influences of impurity in the area of sexual health. We should acknowledge the standard to which Paul called the Thessalonians and make this our standard too.

APPLICATION: SANCTIFIED

- Consider Christians who have been a good example of holiness in their relationships. Thank God for their example and pray that they would continue to be a source of encouragement.

- Reflect on your own attitudes and those highlighted by Paul. Pray for an honourable, other-centred approach to those with whom you have relationship.
- When faced with sexual temptation, pray for the insight to acknowledge your temptation and for the wisdom to pursue holiness instead.

A Quiet Life

Now about your love for one another we do not need to write to you, for you yourselves have been taught by God to love each other. [10] And in fact, you do love all of God's family throughout Macedonia. Yet we urge you, brothers and sisters, to do so more and more, [11] and to make it your ambition to lead a quiet life: You should mind your own business and work with your hands, just as we told you, [12] so that your daily life may win the respect of outsiders and so that you will not be dependent on anybody.

Paul advises the Thessalonians to lead a quiet life a term that comes from the Greek *hesuchazo*, referring to be being at rest, or still. It was often used to allude to the stillness after a storm or the silence that might follow a loud noise.

For Paul to encourage such a way of life seems at odds with his own life. Recall that he had been thrown in prison in Philippi prior to meeting the Thessalonians. He had been bundled away at night from Thessalonica due to unrest and crowds had been agitated in Berea, the next town. Paul was guilty of living anything but a quiet life.

It is true, however, that Paul the missionary was writing a pastoral letter. His purposes in writing were different than his purposes when visiting the Thessalonians in person. In his letter, he gave pastoral advice to those he had left behind to build a church amidst a pagan population. As such, the ministry team needed to be on good terms with those they sought to reach, not constantly at odds with their townsfolk.

This interpretation seems to fit with the rest of the passage, which highlights the importance for Christians to be able to work and not be dependent on others whenever they are able.

Paul encouraged the Thessalonian Christians not to be a source of agitation or unrest. Instead they were to be seen as reliable, hard-working citizens so that they might win the respect of others.

The exhortation to lead a quiet life is a good example of what Jim Petersen would term "lifestyle discipleship." In his book of the same title, he writes that evangelism can be performed through a lifestyle that is lived as a Christian. He argues that such a lifestyle approach can be equally as effective as evangelical events in reaching a generation that is increasing unchurched.[3]

Paul's instruction to lead a quiet life might also have been given out of concern that the Thessalonians, in their enthusiasm for their new belief, could put themselves at risk of persecution. Paul was perhaps anxious that overexuberant expressions of their newfound faith might provoke or exacerbate discrimination

---

3 Jim Peterson, *Lifestyle Discipleship* (Carol Stream, IL: Tyndale House Publisher, 1993).

against the church. It is also possible that Paul was keen for the Thessalonians to adopt appropriate attitudes whilst they awaited the return of Christ. This point is raised later in the letter.

We might reflect on Paul's advice to the Thessalonians as we seek to reach the lost in our own workplaces or neighbourhoods. The wisdom from these verses suggest that we would be better to avoid political agitation and workplace confrontations, where possible, in order to be in a better position to win the respect of others.

APPLICATION: A QUIET LIFE

- Is it your ambition to lead a quiet life? What would such a life look like in your current vocation?
- Can you think of Christians who exemplify the quiet life to which Paul refers? Give thanks for their witness and ask God to bless them.
- Reflect on your life as an evangelistic tool. Ask God to show you how you might use it better for His service.

Rose Again

1 THESSALONIANS 4:13-18

Brothers and sisters, we do not want you to be uninformed about those who sleep in death, so that you do not grieve like the rest of mankind, who have no hope. [14] For we believe that Jesus died and rose again, and so we believe that God will bring with Jesus those who have fallen asleep in him. [15] According to the Lord's word, we tell you that we who are still alive, who are left until the coming of the Lord, will certainly not precede those who have fallen asleep. [16] For the Lord himself will come down from heaven, with a loud command, with the voice of the archangel and with the trumpet call of God, and the dead in Christ will rise first. [17] After that, we who are still alive and are left will be caught up together with them in the clouds to meet the Lord in the air. And so we will be with the Lord forever. [18] Therefore encourage one another with these words.

Paul centres his discussion on the second coming of Christ by reminding the Thessalonians that Christ rose again from the dead.

The Greeks didn't have a word for resurrection (perhaps they were sceptics of this too). Instead the word used here was a composite—*anistemi* (combining *ana* for "again" and *histemi* for "stand").

Jesus stood again after the cross. He was not reincarnated in a different body but arose again as Jesus. Let us consider the concept of Christ rising again from the dead as we reflect on today's reading.

Paul was not troubled by the concept that Christ rose again, for he met with the Lord on the road to Damascus at the time of his conversion (Acts 9). Paul's biography, like those of Peter and James (Jesus's brother), provides strong circumstantial evidence to the Lord's rising again. Along with the horror of the crucifixion, the empty tomb and the early historical accounts all point to the truth of the Lord's rising again. This evidence has helped to convince sceptical journalists, lawyers, and philosophers.

As Christians, we should not be surprised by the resurrection. Once we concede that Jesus is the son of God, we should expect divine miracles to occur. So we marvel at the feeding of the five thousand, walking on water, casting out demons, and the healing of diseases, all of which we accept since they are performed by the Son of God.

Our attitude toward the resurrection should be similar: not to discount the possibility that Christ is capable of such a miraculous sign, through the power of God, simply because He is God. Furthermore, we have the example of Lazarus, which precedes the rising again of Christ (John 11).

As author Paul Beasley Murray wrote, "The resurrection is the first article of the Christian faith and the demonstration of all the rest."[4]

In his discussion of the second coming of Christ, Paul starts from the foundation of the first return. He implores the Thessalonians not to be distracted by the resurrection of Christ but to lead a quiet life and work hard (1 Thessalonians 4:9–12).

He then expresses a similar approach to the equally challenging concept that Christ will return a second time. Christ's second coming was prophesied by Christ Himself in the Olivet discourse in Matthew 24, Mark 13, and Luke 21. Paul's teaching to the Thessalonians mirrors Christ's discourse on the subject.

The appearance of the Lord's own teaching on this matter helps to placate our concerns regarding these difficult to comprehend events. The descriptions in Thessalonians and the gospels belie our own life experiences and would be unbelievable had they not been predicted by Christ, who performed miraculous signs both during His life and at His death, as Paul was keen to remind us.

To the specific concern regarding those Christians who died before Christ returns, the Old Testament describes the resurrection of the dead in Job 19:25–27, Isaiah 26:19, Daniel 12:1, and Psalm 49:15. Paul reassures the Thessalonians that Christians, whether alive or dead, would rise to be with the Lord (1 Thessalonians 4:16–17).

---

4   Paul Beasley Murray, *The Message of the Resurrection* (Leicester, UK: Intervarsity Press, 2000), 17.

Like the Greeks, we might find it difficult to find the words to explain the resurrection or first return, and we would certainly struggle to describe the second coming of Christ. Yet God's promises and those of Christ are true. We therefore must face the certainty of these prophesied events.

Paul hoped that the Thessalonians would not be paralyzed by the unpredictable timing of events, but rather that they would be encouraged. Their encouragement was to be founded on the first return of Jesus and the knowledge that He fulfills His promises.

As we rise again from our beds and go about our daily lives, let us pause on the miracle of the rising again of Christ and let us cling to the hope and encouragement that He has promised to return.

APPLICATION: ROSE AGAIN

- Focussed thought on the resurrection need not be reserved for Easter. Give thanks for the first Easter morning and praise God for His kept promise.
- As you rise from bed this week, take the opportunity to offer a prayer of gratitude for the resurrection or rising again of Christ.
- Thank Jesus for His divine nature, which allows the impossible to become reality.

Children of the Light

1 THESSALONIANS 5:1-11

Now, brothers and sisters, about times and dates we do not need to write to you, [2] for you know very well that the day of the Lord will come like a thief in the night. [3] While people are saying, "Peace and safety," destruction will come on them suddenly, as labor pains on a pregnant woman, and they will not escape.

[4] But you, brothers and sisters, are not in darkness so that this day should surprise you like a thief. [5] You are all children of the light and children of the day. We do not belong to the night or to the darkness. [6] So then, let us not be like others, who are asleep, but let us be awake and sober. [7] For those who sleep, sleep at night, and those who get drunk, get drunk at night. [8] But since we belong to the day, let us be sober, putting on faith and love as a breastplate, and the hope of salvation as a helmet. [9] For God did not appoint us to suffer wrath but to receive salvation through our Lord Jesus Christ. [10] He died for us so that, whether we are awake or asleep, we may live together with him. [11] Therefore encourage one another and build each other up, just as in fact you are doing.

W e will focus our thoughts from these verse on the phrases *"children of the light and children of the day."* The original Greek passage would have been translated as "sons of the light and sons of the day." The phrase "sons of" was used to describe an individual's devotedness to a task, belief, or subject. We can call to mind the time when Jesus referred to James and John as *"sons of thunder"* (Mark 3:17), due to their tempestuous natures.

Paul refers to the Thessalonians using this delightful phrase, "children of the light," and then repeats a similar description, "children of the day" to emphasize it. This implies that the Thessalonians had received knowledge or insight. In the context of the passage, this refers to both a revelation of spiritual issues and an insight into Christ's return.

The link between light and spiritual enlightenment is a common association in the Bible. We might reflect on Paul's own life to illustrate the difference between a child of the light and one of the dark. Prior to his conversion, Paul would have been considered to have been a child of the dark, living in the night, without comprehension of the spiritual world. His existence was like that of a drunk or a sleepwalker who is blind to the realities occurring around him.

At his conversion, he was confronted by the light, physically and spiritually, and became startlingly aware of the judgment of God. Christ's own words confronted him (Acts 9:4). Suddenly aware of God's judgment, Paul was tasked with either following Christ's command, to go into the city and receive instruction, or refusing.

We too face a similar decision. Once we perceive that God is real, and his judgment is close, we have to decide whether to listen to this revelation or ignore it.

God has a role in bringing us into the light. He reveals Himself to us through His creation (Romans 1) and through personal revelation—perhaps in less dramatic ways than He did with Paul, but still in a meaningful and direct manner. When we begin to see the reality of God and accept the implications of who Jesus was, we either step into the light or scurry back into the shadows.

Thankfully for us, Paul did the former and pursued the light with vigour.

Our own steps into the light are also important. By walking toward the light, we acknowledge the proximity of His judgment, understanding our need for salvation and our own inadequacies to prevent our condemnation. Our steps toward the light are our first steps of spiritual obedience to live as children of the light.

When Paul called the Thessalonians children of the day, it might be taken as a simple repetition to emphasize one's transition into a life of light. Since we have received and accepted God's revelation of Jesus as His Son, we now live in the day. Our spiritual lives are not lived out in the dark of night but the light of day. Being children of the day, all that we do is done in the light of Jesus's life, death, and resurrection.

When the subject of Jesus's return arises, Paul encourages the Thessalonian Christians to continue to live as children of the day and not be burdened with anxiety and concern over matters they cannot control or influence. His teaching is a mirror of Christ's own remarks (Mark 13).

The prospect of Christ's return is not intended to be a distraction that captivates our interest. Rather, it is a prophecy spoken of by Christ, meant as an encouragement to the purposes of God and as a reminder of the reasons we need to be children of the light (1 Thessalonians 5:11).

APPLICATION:
CHILDREN OF THE LIGHT

- When you turn on a light today, take a moment to thank God for His grace which enables to you to understand who Jesus was.
- Consider what others might call you a "child of." Are you a child of thunder or of the light?
- Pray that you might live in the day. Having been brought out of the dark, let us not retract into the shadows.

Do Not Quench

1 THESSALONIANS 5:12–22

Now we ask you, brothers and sisters, to acknowledge those who work hard among you, who care for you in the Lord and who admonish you. [13] Hold them in the highest regard in love because of their work. Live in peace with each other. [14] And we urge you, brothers and sisters, warn those who are idle and disruptive, encourage the disheartened, help the weak, be patient with everyone. [15] Make sure that nobody pays back wrong for wrong, but always strive to do what is good for each other and for everyone else.

[16] Rejoice always, [17] pray continually, [18] give thanks in all circumstances; for this is God's will for you in Christ Jesus.

[19] Do not quench the Spirit. [20] Do not treat prophecies with contempt [21] but test them all; hold on to what is good, [22] reject every kind of evil.

Paul's rhetoric in Thessalonians is demonstrative. He encourages and supports the Thessalonian Christians to continue in the vein they has already been practicing. Paul expresses his delight about the way the church has matured, which he attributes to the work of the Holy Spirit and the aptitude of the congregation to accept and receive the Word of God.

As he begins to draw the letter to a close, Paul encourages them in specific areas. In order to address those areas, he provides tools rather than rules.

In particular, Paul urges the Thessalonians to not quench the Spirit's fire (1 Thessalonians 5:19). The original Greek here was *me sbennute*, which translates as "do not put out." Paul was keen that the Thessalonians not suffocate the Spirit's voice in their hearts, for the Spirit itself cannot be extinguished.

But as a result of the gift of free will, we can choose to ignore the Spirit's voice as an influence in our lives. If we ignore the Spirit's influence, we fail to allow ourselves to be guided, directed, and driven by the Spirit's fire. The Spirit in our hearts is like a pilot light in a gas furnace; ideally it serves to set alight our faith and keep it burning.

Paul was earnest in his recommendations concerning the Spirit's leadership, for it was important for his own spiritual health. My sense is that Paul regularly reflected on his lack of spiritual guidance prior to his conversion. He was a living example of the dampened wood that Elijah prepared on Mount Carmen (1 Kings 18). Paul required a spark from God to set the Spirit's fire ablaze in his heart. Sensitive to the many years he had poured water on the work of God's word, Paul was keen that the Spirit's fire be allowed to burn in his heart, having accepted Christ and received the gift of the Spirit. He urged the Thessalonians to do likewise.

Paul's picture that the Thessalonians not quench the Spirit is vivid. I suspect that we have all experienced dreams, passions, and initiatives being quenched. Paul's words encourage us not to see our Christianity in the same way we might look at a new hobby. He urges us to persevere and encourage the Spirit to maintain our Christian faith.

My prayer is that Paul's perspective on this will also be ours. We need to work on the embers of the Spirit so that our faith will burn in our hearts as it did when we first believed.

APPLICATION: DO NOT QUENCH

- If you could see the Spirit's pilot light in your heart, how tall or fired up would it be?
- If acts of faith fuel the Spirit, which acts are you pursuing?
- When you quench your thirst today, take the opportunity to pray that the Spirit continues to burn in your heart.

Grace With

1 THESSALONIANS 5:23-28

May God himself, the God of peace, sanctify you through and through. May your whole spirit, soul and body be kept blameless at the coming of our Lord Jesus Christ. [24] The one who calls you is faithful, and he will do it.

[25] Brothers and sisters, pray for us. [26] Greet all God's people with a holy kiss. [27] I charge you before the Lord to have this letter read to all the brothers and sisters.

[28] The grace of our Lord Jesus Christ be with you.

At the beginning of this book, we reflected on how as Christians we should seek to inspire other Christians. We acknowledged that Paul, Silas, and Timothy nurtured the Thessalonian church in their letter through support and encouragement.

Now we come to the end of 1 Thessalonians and see the authors signing off with a prayer that Christ's grace be with them in their church and personal interactions.

When we consider the potential themes of the letter—political unrest versus the exhortation to live a quiet life, the following of personal desires versus sexual propriety, or stagnating due to a misplaced emphasis in the second coming—we might expect the authors to sign off with detailed instruction on how to avoid these potential pitfalls.

Instead we read a farewell prayer: *"The grace of our Lord Jesus Christ be with you."*

Grace is the unwarranted gift of mercy or forgiveness and was recognized in Greek culture. The giver of a gracious act was commended and held in high esteem since such an act went above and beyond the expected social and cultural norms.

Grace goes beyond altruism, which is an act performed without the expectation of receiving anything in return. A graceful action is one that displays mercy and/or forgiveness and is generous in its relief. Nowhere is this better appreciated than in the act of God to give His Son to be incarnated, live amongst men, be crucified, and then rise again so that we might believe and be received into His kingdom.

As Christians we recognize that we don't deserve God's favour or acceptance, yet through the work of Christ and God's grace we can become children of God—blessed, forgiven and received. It is this grace with which Paul began the letter (1 Thessalonians 1:1), and he returns to it in the final verses.

Paul chooses to use the small word "with" to describe a profound relationship. This is a preposition that we can readily pass over, for we perceive it to merely link phrases without carrying any real weight in a sentence. In Greek, it was the word *meta*, which translates as "amidst or amongst."

The perspective here is that God's grace is not a distant sidekick accompanying us on our adventures as Christians. Christ's

39

grace is instead an all-pervading, all-consuming presence, a true companion that melts our cold hearts and inspires our thoughts and actions.

Paul prayed as he finished writing that grace would be prevalent through the church, surrounding it and suffusing it. It was his prayer that grace would be amongst the church and be readily apparent in the people's interactions with one another and their community. The presence of their grace would be like a warm breeze on a summer's evening, refreshingly temperate to ward off the chill of night.

He saw the continued adoption of grace as a key to the ongoing growth and success of the Thessalonian church. Throughout the letter, Paul had been complimentary toward the church, if not surprised by their progress. Yet he reminded them to continue to embrace Christ's grace.

Christ's grace is captivating and awe-inspiring. Reflecting on Jesus's life and drawing on the strength of His Spirit can move us to act with grace we didn't think possible.

Paul encourages the Thessalonians to move beyond acts and develop a lifestyle that is pervaded by grace—a life that is grace-with and not just grace-punctuated, a life where uncharacteristic mercy and forgiveness are second nature rather than second thoughts.

Let us pray that these verses Paul closes with be true for ourselves and our own churches, so that we too might surprise Paul just like the Thessalonians did.

APPLICATION: GRACE WITH

- Consider what a grace-with life would look like for your church. Pray that God would enable this vision.
- How might we as individuals become more grace-with, where grace becomes second nature?
- When you encounter the word "with" today, take a moment to remember Paul's prayer.

Reflections

1 THESSALONIANS

We always thank God for all of you and continually mention you in our prayers.

—1 Thessalonians 1:2

This letter from Paul, Silas, and Timothy is full of affection for a group of people who became Christians under trying circumstances over a short ministry period. The tone of the writing is encouraging and the recipients are frequently complimented.

While reading these passages, I found myself questioning my attitudes toward other Christians. My attitudes ought to be more like those of the authors—more appreciative of, and thankful for, my fellow Christians.

Paul writes that Timothy returned to Thessalonica to support and encourage the believers there. This seems like a good model to imitate. With thought, multiple ways can be found to affirm Christians we know, whether in prayer or physically in person, by simply spending time with them. The implication from Thessalonians is that profound value is to be found in upholding one another.

This renewed understanding of the value of fellow Christians also comes across in the way Paul thanks God for the

Thessalonians. Paul was speechless to express just how grateful he felt to God for saving them.

His attitude provides us with an appreciation of what it means for others to be saved. It would have been apparent to Paul just how miraculous conversion to Christianity is, given his dramatic conversion. His arresting experience on the road to Damascus likely influenced his profound gratitude to God for the willingness of the Thessalonians to receive the gospel.

Our conversion experiences are likely less dramatic than Paul's, and consequently our attitudes concerning the conversion of other Christians today are likely different. We might not consider such salvation experiences to be miracles in the same way as we think of the feeding of the five thousand, yet they are miraculous events. In fact, they are even more miraculous today given our increasingly secular culture and lack of Christian literacy in society.

Thinking of our fellow Christians as being miracles of God has changed my perception, and hopefully my interactions, with people both at church and at home. People in chairs or pews around us on Sunday, in Paul's eyes, are gifts from the Father. We are to appreciate them in recognition of His heavenly mercy and power. If we are fortunate to have family members who are also Christians, Paul would encourage us to pray to God and express our thanks for them, even if we cannot find the words.

I do wonder whether it would be easier to have more grace toward one another if we were more thankful for one another. Ideally, we would then come close to the "grace-with" attitude that is noted in this letter's final passage.

It is our hoped that through this examination of 1 Thessalonians, your perceptions of other Christians have shifted. This may not happen overnight, for relationships can be complex. However, Paul, Silas, and Timothy would call us to begin by being more thankful for one another, thankful to God for bringing others into our sphere, and thankful to them for simply persisting, enduring, and hopefully thriving in their Christianity, like the Thessalonians.

Introduction

2 THESSALONIANS

Written shortly after 1 Thessalonians, this second letter is a three-chapter postscript. Penned by the same three authors—Paul, Silas, and Timothy—it discusses issues raised in the first letter in greater detail. The rationale for the letter may have been due to changing circumstances in the church or in response to the discussions between Timothy and the others subsequent to his return from Thessalonica.

Paul is believed to have written the letter on behalf of his fellow evangelists in Corinth around 52 AD. During this time, Paul, Silas, and Timothy were still in the midst of Paul's second missionary journey and occupied by establishing the Corinthian church and presumably being hard at work. It was a busy but fruitful time one for the church, and Paul continues in this letter to express how the Thessalonian church is a steadfast source of encouragement.

Paul will discuss more details concerning the coming, or *parousia*, of Jesus. This is the Greek word for "arrival." In Latin, we know it as *adventus*, which in English is called advent. In Christian parlance, *parousia* has become synonymous with the second coming. We tend to reserve the term advent for the first coming. It's used in the church calendar to celebrate the twenty-four days prior to Christmas.

Paul discusses the importance of demonstrating a responsible spiritual attitude as the Thessalonians await the *parousia*. He also draws on the promise of the return of Christ to bolster the church as it faces persecution.

Both these themes have relevance to twenty-first-century Christians.

The promise of Christ's return is not an easy topic of conversation amongst Christians, since it stretches our enlightened scientific minds to consider a world outside the tangible.

Paul found similar challenges in discussing this prophecy in his first letter and encouraged the Thessalonians to rely on the foundation of the resurrection of Christ. He argued that if this seemingly impossible event had occurred, would it not be possible for other miraculous events to occur in the future? Thus, the *parousia* becomes a future reality, and as a reality it should continue to inspire people's attitudes, perseverance, and endurance.

Although we too may be stretched by the concept of Christ's return, this was His promise. If we are willing to trust His promises, we too will find inspiration from them and from Paul's words in 2 Thessalonians.

Give Thanks

2 THESSALONIANS 1:1-12

Paul, Silas and Timothy,

To the church of the Thessalonians in God our Father and the Lord Jesus Christ:

[2] Grace and peace to you from God the Father and the Lord Jesus Christ.

[3] We ought always to thank God for you, brothers and sisters, and rightly so, because your faith is growing more and more, and the love all of you have for one another is increasing. [4] Therefore, among God's churches we boast about your perseverance and faith in all the persecutions and trials you are enduring.

[5] All this is evidence that God's judgment is right, and as a result you will be counted worthy of the kingdom of God, for which you are suffering. [6] God is just: He will pay back trouble to those who trouble you [7] and give relief to you who are troubled, and to us as well. This will happen when the Lord Jesus is revealed from heaven in blazing fire with his powerful angels. [8] He will punish those who do not know God and do not obey the gospel of our Lord Jesus. [9] They will be punished with everlasting destruction and shut out

from the presence of the Lord and from the glory of his might ¹⁰ on the day he comes to be glorified in his holy people and to be marveled at among all those who have believed. This includes you, because you believed our testimony to you.

¹¹ With this in mind, we constantly pray for you, that our God may make you worthy of his calling, and that by his power he may bring to fruition your every desire for goodness and your every deed prompted by faith. ¹² We pray this so that the name of our Lord Jesus may be glorified in you, and you in him, according to the grace of our God and the Lord Jesus Christ.

The letter begins with a thank you to God (2 Thessalonians 1:3). The Greek word used is *eucharisteo*—from *eu*, meaning "well," and *charizomai*, meaning "to give or grant." A literal translation would be "to demonstrate wellness or thankfulness." It is the title used for communion services in Anglican churches, services which give thanks to God for Jesus. Here the authors are giving thanks to God for the Thessalonians.

Always giving thanks to God was a way to remind Paul and his co-workers of the significance of the Thessalonians. The church in Thessalonica had embraced the message that had been preached to them. In Paul's eyes, this was no small feat. To turn from secularism to Christianity was a miracle that required God to work in the minds and hearts of those who had heard the gospel.

It is to God that the authors therefore direct their thanks, mindful of His work in the lives of those who had been converted.

We know that Paul was also thankful to God for the continued witness of the Thessalonian church. The way they lived their lives reflected their decision to turn from worldly philosophy and follow Jesus.

The strength of witness of the Thessalonian church was a source of encouragement to Paul. There is almost a note of surprise in the tone of 1 Thessalonians in response to just how much the converts had grown in their faith. Here Paul gives thanks again not only for their conversion but their persistence in their new lives, growing in love and faith (2 Thessalonians 1:3).

Other topics are introduced in these initial verses concerning persecution and the second coming of Christ. These topics are developed by Paul as the letter progresses and we will consider them too.

At the beginning of this letter, however, Paul pauses, poignantly perhaps, to thank God again and again for the Thessalonians. He was deeply appreciative that the gospel had resonated in their hearts. The reverberations from their earlier reception of God's wisdom were a source of perpetual inspiration for Paul.

Let us also pause and give thanks to God for those whom we have fellowship with in Christ, whether they be our church leaders, our fellow brothers or sisters in Christ, or those we seek to reach. Give thanks to God for each of these groups and ask Him to continue to lead them to a greater understanding of His ways.

APPLICATION: GIVE THANKS

- Take a moment to give thanks to God for those around you who support you in your faith.
- Consider those Christians who are more distant from you at the moment. Thank God for the times when you were close and ask Him to bless them.
- Thank God for the privilege it is to know Him as our Father and to know His Son as our saviour.

The Truth

2 THESSALONIANS 2:1–12

Concerning the coming of our Lord Jesus Christ and our being gathered to him, we ask you, brothers and sisters, [2] not to become easily unsettled or alarmed by the teaching allegedly from us—whether by a prophecy or by word of mouth or by letter—asserting that the day of the Lord has already come. [3] Don't let anyone deceive you in any way, for that day will not come until the rebellion occurs and the man of lawlessness is revealed, the man doomed to destruction. [4] He will oppose and will exalt himself over everything that is called God or is worshiped, so that he sets himself up in God's temple, proclaiming himself to be God.

[5] Don't you remember that when I was with you I used to tell you these things? [6] And now you know what is holding him back, so that he may be revealed at the proper time. [7] For the secret power of lawlessness is already at work; but the one who now holds it back will continue to do so till he is taken out of the way. [8] And then the lawless one will be revealed, whom the Lord Jesus will overthrow with the breath of his mouth and destroy by the splendor of his coming. [9] The coming

of the lawless one will be in accordance with how Satan works. He will use all sorts of displays of power through signs and wonders that serve the lie, [10] and all the ways that wickedness deceives those who are perishing. They perish because they refused to love the truth and so be saved. [11] For this reason God sends them a powerful delusion so that they will believe the lie [12] and so that all will be condemned who have not believed the truth but have delighted in wickedness.

Paul, Silas, and Timothy brought the truth to the Thessalonians concerning the gospel. Others were apparently peddling untruths and lies concerning the life and promises of Christ, and these distracted the Thessalonians.

The gospel told by the apostle and his fellow evangelists included the news regarding the second coming of Jesus (2 Thessalonians 2:5). The return of Jesus is an aspect of the gospel that isn't told much in modern times. It is rarely the focus of gospel outreach.

In completeness, however, the gospel is the telling of Jesus's remarkable life, with His teachings and miracles. It is the story of His tragic death that bought justice for our sins. It is the amazing history of His resurrection and post-crucifixion appearances that changed the lives of sceptics, deserters, and persecutors. It is the description of the gift of the Holy Spirit given to those who accept Jesus as Lord over their lives. Finally, it is His promise to return in a glorious second appearance, also known as the *parousia*.

In this complete story, there are several points at which individuals might experience salvation. Exactly how we experience salvation can vary and it depends somewhat on what we perceive as the most perilous thing from which we need to be saved.

In acknowledging the existence of Christ and the wisdom of His teachings, we can be saved from ourselves. We are saved from a life we might have lived to a life with less conflict, hatred, and anger, moving to a life of belief in Christ typified by appreciation, thanks, and positive attitudes.

In recognition of His traumatic death, we may be confronted by wrongs in our own lives. Christ's suffering may provide motivation for us to be introspective about ourselves, our selfishness, and our pride. We might find ourselves being provoked to take ourselves away from those bleak and dark thoughts and actions. Instead we may be said to have been saved by the cross to live with Christ in a godlier fashion.

Alternatively, we might understand our salvation as meaning that we've been saved from death and eternal judgment by believing in Christ's resurrection. This is often the aspect of salvation we focus on in our churches. As Christians, we have been saved to eternal life and preserved from God's wrath.

The Holy Spirit might be a focus for others. By knowing they have received this precious gift as a seal of His promise, they acknowledge that their salvation has occurred.

Finally, a few will contemplate salvation as Christ's promised second coming, at which time the church will be called to Him and a new Earth will be born. The promise of the new Earth becomes the saving promise and is elevated in the minds of these believers as the most critical salvation message.

It seems that some in the Thessalonian church had listened to preaching expressing that Christ had already returned. It is difficult not to blame them for their enthusiasm to embrace the spiritual and live with anticipation of God's next breakthrough. There is a sense that their misdirection was born from the depth of their belief in the gospel. They were committed and convicted of its truth and sought to lead their lives in readiness of Christ's final glorious return. Thus, amongst the celebration and euphoria that God had broken through the heavens and revealed His Son, making salvation possible to all, some of the Thessalonians came to believe that the next chapter was imminent.

This misguided proportion of the church hadn't held to the truth that Paul and his team had taught. Rather they had been persuaded by the charismatic lies of others (2 Thessalonians 2:2–3). In this, Paul had to remind them to love the truth (2 Thessalonians 2:10–12).

The Greek word for truth is *aletheia*, which translates to "without concealment." Truth conveys unabashed honesty and holds back no detail. It is revelatory in removing any mists or veils of secrecy or deception.

Paul implores the Thessalonians to ensure that they hold to the whole of the gospel story, the whole of salvation narrative as we have reviewed it. This ensure that no one is focussed on just one aspect.

Although we might scoff quietly to ourselves about the basic error of this proportion of the Thessalonian church, we should reflect on whether our own impression of salvation is too focussed.

I suspect we will not have focussed too long on the endtimes like the Thessalonians, but we may have concentrated our thinking on other portions of the gospel. When we do this, we limit the truth and might be guilty of lowering a veil over certain aspects of the gospel.

To be sure that anyone listening to our gospel stories hears the truth, we should include both our favourite aspects as well as those aspects we are less familiar with. Otherwise, our listeners could fall afoul of charlatans who try to sell a different gospel.

APPLICATION: THE TRUTH

- Do you focus on aspects of the gospel—the miracles, the teaching, and the resurrection? Pray that we would understand more of the whole story so that we might acknowledge Christ's legacy with greater appreciation.
- Consider your attitudes toward the second coming of Christ. It was promised by Jesus and accounts of it are found in three gospels. Thank God that He has a plan to save not just His church but also the earth.
- What should our attitude be toward the salvation of earth and Christ's second coming? Paul suggests that we shouldn't absolve ourselves of our current responsibilities. Consider what this means for ourselves and our churches.

Hold Fast

2 THESSALONIANS 2:13–17

But we ought always to thank God for you, brothers and sisters loved by the Lord, because God chose you as firstfruits to be saved through the sanctifying work of the Spirit and through belief in the truth. [14] He called you to this through our gospel, that you might share in the glory of our Lord Jesus Christ.

[15] So then, brothers and sisters, stand firm and hold fast to the teachings we passed on to you, whether by word of mouth or by letter.

[16] May our Lord Jesus Christ himself and God our Father, who loved us and by his grace gave us eternal encouragement and good hope, [17] encourage your hearts and strengthen you in every good deed and word.

Something had begun to undermine the Thessalonians' faith. Like a pebble being thrown into serene waters, ripples of disturbance had spread throughout the church, offsetting their vision of the future and causing them to jostle against each other like boats on a shore caught in the migrating wavelets.

We don't know what it was that unbalanced their equilibrium, but Paul calls them to hold fast to the teachings that were given to them both in person and in his first letter.

The Greek word translated to "hold fast" is *krateo*, which has at its root in the Greek word for strength, *kratos*. Paul urges the Thessalonians to be strong to the teachings or traditions that were handed down personally to them either through in person communication or via personal correspondence.

By placing too much emphasis on lofty prophecies of the second coming of Christ, could it be that the congregation had lost sight, or let go, of the teachings of Paul, Silas, and Timothy? Paul reminds them to be strong in those original teachings, to seize hold of his words and messages lest they be tempted to believe false prophecy or a deceptive gospel.

Paul felt strongly enough about the potential of the Thessalonians to drift into unwholesome lives as a result of whatever teachings they were beginning to listen to that he sent this second letter. It emphasizes having an appropriate attitude to the second coming and on being responsible whilst we wait. Paul encourages his readers to focus on the primary sources for their belief and not be diverted by attractive alternatives that prey on human weaknesses.

From Paul's call to be strong and hold fast to the teachings of trusted sources, or the gospels themselves, we can find a salient message for today. Alternative gospels or teachings that seem attractive are usually false. They can be difficult to appreciate since their rhetoric may be deceptive, and the very nature of deception is that it is hard to spot. If it were easy, we would recognize every lie we encounter. Paul's message is that we should be careful when we hear a new teaching to treat it with some suspicion, especially if it preys on our tendencies to sin.

Some Thessalonians had become lazy and were no longer going to work, for they believed that Christ's return was imminent. Here, the deceit preyed on their human tendency to shy away from work. Thus the teaching that led to this action was attractive to some.

Of course, such deceitful teaching may not be so easy to spot. However, if it preys on our human tendencies of greed, anger, pride, envy or desire, it is likely to be false.

In this, we might recall the algorithms of certain social media platforms that have been found to deliberately target certain emotions in us in order to generate more internet activity.

Let us hold fast to the message of the gospel and of Paul himself from his letters, holding strongly to those teachings and prophecies lest we be tempted by deceptive alternatives.

Paul prayed that Jesus and the Lord God would encourage the Thessalonians to be strong in the way they lived out the gospel (2 Thessalonians 2:16–17). This is an apt prayer to pray for ourselves in an era when we can be easily distracted by so many alternative truths that are readily available via the internet.

APPLICATION: HOLD FAST

- Sometimes we are caught off-balance by changes in society. Pray that in applying Christianity to these issues, we would hold fast to the heart of our faith.

- Ask God to help you see deceit in false teachings, so that you will not be led astray from His word.
- Pray as Paul did that Christ and the Father would encourage your heart to be strong in word and deed so you can hold fast to the gospel.

Perseverance

As for other matters, brothers and sisters, pray for us that the message of the Lord may spread rapidly and be honored, just as it was with you. ² And pray that we may be delivered from wicked and evil people, for not everyone has faith. ³ But the Lord is faithful, and he will strengthen you and protect you from the evil one. ⁴ We have confidence in the Lord that you are doing and will continue to do the things we command. ⁵ May the Lord direct your hearts into God's love and Christ's perseverance.

Some in the Thessalonian church had become preoccupied with Jesus's second coming and their salvation. In this passage, Paul prays into this potentially damaging captivation. It's an abbreviated "Lord's prayer" in which he asks that the Lord's will be done on earth as it is in heaven, calling for the message to spread rapidly (2 Thessalonians 3:1).

Paul reminds the church that God supplies their daily bread and will uphold them through His faithfulness and by giving them strength (2 Thessalonians 3:3). He asks that they not be led into temptation, but rather that they be protected from it (2

Thessalonians 3:3) and delivered from evil (2 Thessalonians 3:2). Paul then reminds them that they can have confidence in God's kingdom, His sovereignty, just as Paul has confidence that God will see through what He has begun in Thessalonica (2 Thessalonians 3:4).

Finally, Paul reminds them this relationship is forever and ever, underpinned by the steadfastness of Christ's perseverance and God's everlasting love.

These verses thus bear a remarkable similarity to the text of Matthew 6:9–13, which on the one hand is perhaps not surprising since Christ taught His followers to pray like this. On the other hand, though, it is wonderful to see the structure adopted by Paul as he speaks to his dear Thessalonians. Paul uses these pointed words to address them in personal tones, conveying his deep conviction that the Thessalonians, with God's strength and guidance, will overcome their current struggles.

Paul ends his prayer by mentioning Christ's perseverance. We might mistakenly think he was suggesting that Christ needs a lot of perseverance given that He is working with such a collection of inept disciples, like us and the Thessalonians. Whilst there is truth in the fact that we are all far from perfect, and that we rely on Christ's grace for our continued nurturing, this was not Paul's meaning. Rather, he was calling the Thessalonians to direct their hearts to have Christlike perseverance. The Thessalonians were being encouraged to develop an unshakable faith to do God's will.

Perseverance is translated from the Greek word *hupomone*, which some translations have rendered as "steadfastness." The Greek is constructed from the words *hupo* and *meno*, meaning "under" and "remain" respectively. We are then to mimic Christ's attitude to remain under or in submission as well. In this, we should note the strength implied by the concept of remaining. To remain is to resist forces that would seek to bring change. There is no flaky, shaky attitude to being under constant pressure when we display Christlike perseverance.

There is also no whining, groaning, or creaking at the weight of the thing under which we are bearing up. Christlike perseverance is a special quality, and it is what some elements of the Thessalonian church needed in a generous measure. Some had stopped persevering, believing that the day of the Lord had already come (2 Thessalonians 2:2). Others had become nonchalant about their responsibilities (2 Thessalonians 3:6), perhaps in light of the promised second coming. Still others had given up working (2 Thessalonians 3:11).

Paul urged them to step back into their Christian disciplines and prayed that Christlike perseverance might enable them to do so. When we consider Christlike perseverance in these contexts, it becomes an attractive and universally appealing characteristic, akin to courage.

APPLICATION: PERSEVERANCE

- Christ's perseverance to do the Father's will bought salvation for the Thessalonians and ourselves. Thank Him for His endurance.

- Pray that our own perseverance will not just be alloyed with His, but rather replaced by His, which is better by far.
- Consider those you know who are under pressure at the moment. Pray that they might receive Christlike perseverance to enable their triumphant endurance.

Teachings

2 THESSALONIANS 3:6-15

In the name of the Lord Jesus Christ, we command you, brothers and sisters, to keep away from every believer who is idle and disruptive and does not live according to the teaching you received from us. [7] For you yourselves know how you ought to follow our example. We were not idle when we were with you, [8] nor did we eat anyone's food without paying for it. On the contrary, we worked night and day, laboring and toiling so that we would not be a burden to any of you. [9] We did this, not because we do not have the right to such help, but in order to offer ourselves as a model for you to imitate. [10] For even when we were with you, we gave you this rule: "The one who is unwilling to work shall not eat."

[11] We hear that some among you are idle and disruptive. They are not busy; they are busybodies. [12] Such people we command and urge in the Lord Jesus Christ to settle down and earn the food they eat. [13] And as for you, brothers and sisters, never tire of doing what is good.

[14] Take special note of anyone who does not obey our instruction in this letter. Do not associate with them, in order that they may feel ashamed. [15] Yet do not

regard them as an enemy, but warn them as you would a fellow believer.

Paul encouraged the church in 2 Thessalonians 2:15 to hold on to the teachings they were given, whether in person or by letter. In today's verses, he does so again through criticism of those who rejected the teachings of Paul, Silas, and Timothy (2 Thessalonians 3:6). The word teaching comes from the Greek *paradosis*, which could be translated as "tradition," since it is derived from *paradidomi*, which implies in-person or delivered teaching. Paul is calling the Thessalonians not to replace the traditions they received with false teaching.

As we have seen throughout 1 and 2 Thessalonians, there was a personal connection between the congregation in Thessalonica and the disciples, belying the brief amount of time the disciples spent there. We are given a surprising sense of an intimacy of understanding between the church and their teachers.

The familiarity, though, stems from the joy Paul feels about the church. He is pleased with their continued progress in ministry, progress that has been made even in his absence, and after such a short mission experience. His pleasure is built on the evidence of their faith.

Remember that Paul had sent Timothy on a reconnaissance trip to see how the church was doing. Timothy's report evidently filled Paul with unexpected hope that the Thessalonians had grasped the essence of the gospel and were flourishing under the Holy Spirit's guidance. The flourishing nature of the congregation had built up a rapport in Paul's heart, one which he communicates several times throughout 1 and 2 Thessalonians.

There was concern, though, that an element of the church was rejecting the personal touches of the disciples' instruction. This group wasn't adhering to the teaching they had been given. They were in essence rejecting the personal, family-like ministry of the disciples, cutting off the intimacy that had been extended to them and under which others of the church were still flourishing.

The insistence of some to reject the personal ministry of the disciples was causing them to adopt offbeat beliefs. This group was following the beat of a different rhythm, one that didn't keep time with the church's mainstream. It was offbeat with the gospel and ultimately not in keeping with God's desire for their lives.

The implication of 2 Thessalonians 3:6–13 is that for some reason this group had developed an unhealthy attitude toward labour. This attitude wasn't one they had been taught by the disciples (2 Thessalonians 3:7).

In the past, commentators have associated the perceived unhealthy attitude toward work with a misunderstanding regarding the timing of the second coming of Christ (2 Thessalonians 2). In keeping with this opinion, the group was out of time with the rhythm of the church and out of time with God's plans for Christ's return.

Whether we should associate the two criticisms—beliefs surrounding work and the second coming—is less relevant than Paul's assertion here that the Thessalonians should live according to the teaching they received in person from the disciples.

We too are called to live in accordance with the teachings of the disciples and Christ. Whilst we have not had the privilege of receiving these directly, we can still benefit, like the Thessalonians, from Paul's letters.

Our attitudes toward work should reflect those of Paul and his coworkers. Even with the passage of time, the verses remain true: the tone we set through our work can demonstrate our self-discipline, which reflects on our relationship with God. God does not call us to act with selfish ambition (Philippians 2:3–4), but we are called to do the good works which God prepared in advanced for us to do (Ephesians 2:10).

Perhaps the intimacy Paul felt toward the Thessalonians underpins some of his tone in these verses. Maybe he was affected by the rejection by some of his personal assertions regarding the appropriate conduct of labour.

Therefore, Paul writes to remind the people of the intimacy of his teaching and to appeal for them to return to the fold. His hope is that they may flourish like the rest of the congregation.

I suspect he would make the same appeal to us were we offbeat with our church and ignoring salient lessons from the Bible.

APPLICATION: TEACHINGS

- Paul's appeal to the Thessalonians should ring true for us; we ignore his teachings at our own peril. Pray that we would be open to hear what God would teach us through His word.

- What do you think about Paul's attitude to work and his rather blunt assertion that a man who is unwilling to work shall not eat?
- There is a balance to be struck when managing these teachings from Paul lest we be unkind to those who are too infirm or frail to work. Pray that God would help you to find the path to navigate this.

Peace

2 THESSALONIANS 3:16-18

Now may the Lord of peace himself give you peace at all times and in every way. The Lord be with all of you.

[17] I, Paul, write this greeting in my own hand, which is the distinguishing mark in all my letters. This is how I write.

[18] The grace of our Lord Jesus Christ be with you all.

Paul closes his second letter to the Thessalonians with a benediction and a flourish of his own handwriting. His final message is for the Thessalonians to dwell in the peace that comes from knowing Christ.

This was my hope at the start of this series of books, that they would encourage readers to spend more time enjoying Christ's peace, by taking a word from each reading and holding it front and centre through the routines of daily life.

Peace that comes from knowing Christ is a central part of the attraction of Christianity. At this point in the letter, the notion of peace should be distinguished from the idleness which Paul has been railing against in the preceding verses. The peace Paul wishes for the Thessalonians is not a satiated desire that leaves them unmotivated and lazy. Rather, it is a core sense of security and significance that provides them with the quiet confidence to pursue a godly life.

Peace from Christ was the topic of Jesus's address to the disciples at the last supper (John 14). He promised not to leave them, and by extension us, as orphans but to grant them peace. He gives this gift not as a reward or piecemeal, as the world might do, but generously and with grace.

Christ achieves this generosity through His life, death, and resurrection, as well as His gift of the Holy Spirit and through His promise to return.

As a result, our salvation, or peace, is granted in several ways. We are granted salvation and therefore peace through His saving grace in our lives. We are saved from the life of sin we might have led. We are also saved from death; with Jesus's resurrection the promise is given that we will not receive eternal damnation but rather be granted life in heaven and on the new earth. We are thus saved from the natural disasters that will beset our earthly home, for according to His prophecy the new earth will be born with His second coming.

Finally, and often importantly for Christians, Christ saves us from carrying bitterness and hurt throughout our lives. Through His love we are able to forgive and let go of our bitterness, to be freed to do His will without the burden of internal conflicts or harboured anger.

The peace of Christ speaks to His saving grace in all these ways, and it was significant for Paul to remind the Thessalonians of this as he signed off. Centring themselves on Christ's peace would have drawn the Thessalonians to focus on the breadth and depth of Christ's salvation. Christ's peace did not just grant salvation for this life; it was also for the future. It was not just for individuals, but for the whole world.

As we complete our study of Thessalonians, we are reminded of the challenges presented with the second coming, and with the challenges of being too relaxed or lazy. Paul, faithful to his role as pastor, reminds us to dwell in peace and recall the settling calm that comes from knowing Jesus, the Lord of peace.

Whatever theological or practical challenges our churches may struggle with, Christ's peace is sufficient to provide a balm to soothe and restore. We would do well to remain in it a while longer during our daily routines.

APPLICATION: PEACE

- Reflect on what Christ's peace means to you. Do you experience His peace and see it as a reassurance of your salvation?
- How can being at peace be empowering? Contrast this with the warning against idleness which some resort to in response to salvation. Pray for wisdom to choose peace that leads to fulfillment rather than a satiated sense which makes us lazy.
- Pray that Christ's peace might be more than a fleeting notion but that it could become a reservoir of relief which you can call upon.

Reflections

2 THESSALONIANS

We were not idle when we were with you…

—2 Thessalonians 3:7

2 Thessalonians serves as a long postscript to 1 Thessalonians, perhaps written following a more in-depth debriefing of Timothy's report. There remains a strong supportive flavour to the letter. Whatever Timothy revealed, the Thessalonians were still dear to Paul. They also remained a source of encouragement. Paul was pleased at the way they had run with their faith to establish a mature congregation.

There is also a sternness to the letter that wasn't appreciated in 1 Thessalonians. Paul wishes to be clear about the appropriate attitudes toward the second coming. He urges the Thessalonians not to be distracted by other teachings but to remain with the lessons given by himself, Silas, and Timothy. He gives strong direction on how the Thessalonians should act with respect to working, decrying idleness and encouraging labour with unequivocal language.

I was prompted by Paul's words to reflect on whether idleness had crept into my own Christian life. Had I begun to wallow in the peace of my salvation like I might slip into a hot bath? Perhaps I was enjoying the pleasant warmth and satisfied emotion too much. Did I need to use the restored feelings and sense of peace Christ brings to be more active in the church?

I think this was the rub to 2 Thessalonians for me: Paul saying, "Do not be idle with your salvation. Seek the peace of Christ, but labour in your salvation to be sanctified so that His peace might prevail in you at all times."

For Further Reading

Michael W. Holmes, *1 & 2 Thessalonians: NIV Application Commentary* (Grand Rapids, MI: Zondervan, 1998).

William Barclay, *The Letters to the Philippians, Colossians and Thessalonians: The New Daily Study Bible* (Louisville, KY: Westminster John Knox Press, 2003).

The Greek translations in this book have been paraphrased from material found at: "Verse by Verse Commentary by Book," *Precept Austin*. Date of access: August 3, 2022 (www.preceptaustin.org/verse_by_verse).

For Further Reading

Proceeds from the sales of this book will be donated to St. Timothy's Christian Classical Academy, Ottawa and LOCAL Church, Ottawa.

ST. TIMOTHY'S CHRISTIAN CLASSICAL ACADEMY, OTTAWA

St. Timothy's is a small interdenominational Christian school for seventy to eighty pupils from Senior Kindergarten to Grade Eight. It was founded by a group of families in 2005 and has grown to its current size over the past seventeen years. It is a charitable organization and seeks to offer classical education in a Christian environment to children from a broad range of backgrounds. This is achieved through generous provision of tuition assistance.

The dedicated faculty at St Timothy's seek to lead their students to revere truth, desire goodness, and rejoice in beauty. The school has been housed in several locations throughout Ottawa since its inception but would ideally seek to establish a home for itself.

In the meantime, the school continues to be a beacon for Christ in the inner city. St. Timothy's strives to bless children, parents, and broader community so as to fulfill the ambassadorial role that Paul strove for in his pupil Timothy.

Further details can be found online: www.st-timothys.ca

LOCAL CHURCH, OTTAWA

LOCAL Church is spread over four campuses across southern Ontario—in Kingston, Ottawa, Toronto, and online. It is a young church and was founded by pastors Levi and Nadia Marychurch, who emigrated from New Zealand to Canada in 2018.

LOCAL Church seeks to foster a community feel in whichever campus one attends. The congregations come from diverse backgrounds, with a significant proportion of attendees being young adults and students.

The church preaches and professes a Christ-focused message. It has generous ministries in local and international charitable giving. LOCAL vigorously promotes the benefits of small group discipleship ministry.

More details of the ministry and work of the church can be found online: www.localchurch.co

A WORD FROM HIS WORD
BY GARY R. SMALL

Each chapter of *A Word from His Word* focuses on a single word or phrase from a short biblical passage. It is the author's prayer that by returning to a simplified but effective approach to Bible reading, your daily times with God's word will be invigorated. Enjoy the entire series!

Now available:

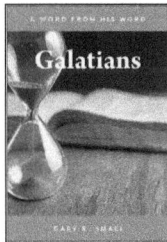

| Galatians | Philippians |
| Ephesians | Colossians |

Coming soon:

Romans	1 & 2 Timothy
1 Corinthians	Philemon & Titus
2 Corinthians